IMAGES
of America

BOSTON'S FENWAY

D1609414

Ted Williams and Babe Ruth, although on opposite baseball teams, shake one another's hand at Boston's Fenway Park on July 17, 1943. These two men became legends in their own time, and although Babe Ruth wears the uniform of the New York Yankees, he actually began his illustrious baseball career with the Boston Red Sox, playing for the team from 1914 to 1919.

I see great things in baseball. It's our game—the American game. It will take our people out-of-doors, fill them with oxygen, give them a larger physical stoicism. Tend to relieve us from being a nerveous, dyseptic set. Repair these losses, and be a blessing to us.

—Walt Whitman

IMAGES
of America

BOSTON'S FENWAY

Anthony Mitchell Sammarco

ARCADIA

Copyright © 2002 by Anthony Mitchell Sammarco.
ISBN 0-7385-1126-9

First printed in 2002.

Published by Arcadia Publishing,
an imprint of Tempus Publishing, Inc.
2A Cumberland Street
Charleston, SC 29401

Printed in Great Britain.

Library of Congress Catalog Card Number: 2002110444

For all general information contact Arcadia Publishing at:
Telephone 843-853-2070
Fax 843-853-0044
E-Mail sales@arcadiapublishing.com

For customer service and orders:
Toll-Free 1-888-313-2665

Visit us on the internet at http://www.arcadiapublishing.com

Boston's Symphony Hall, designed by Charles McKim of the noted architectural firm of McKim, Mead & White, was built in 1900 at the corner of Huntington and Massachusetts Avenues in the Fenway of Boston. The symphony orchestra was established in 1881 through the efforts of prominent Bostonian Henry Lee Higginson, and the early concerts were held in the Boston Music Hall on Hamilton Place off Tremont Street. The present Symphony Hall, with its impressive colonnade of engaged Ionic columns facing Huntington Avenue, became in 1900 the new home of not only the Boston Symphony Orchestra but also of the Boston Pops and the Handel and Haydn Society. It is considered one of the most acoustically perfect spaces in Boston.

CONTENTS

In this view looking east on Huntington Avenue in 1950, street traffic awaits the changing traffic light at Ginsborough Street in the foreground. On the far left are the dome of the Mother Church of the First Church of Christ, Scientist and Symphony Hall. In the center distance rises the tower of the New England Mutual Life Insurance Company (now known as the New England), which was designed by Cram & Ferguson and completed in 1942. On the right is the old John Hancock Building, designed by Parker, Thomas & Rice and built in 1924. Its Art Deco tower was designed by Cram & Ferguson and built in 1950. The tower served as the Back Bay's first high-rise office building (although, in 1895, Haddon Hall became the first building in the Back Bay to break the height restrictions), and its beacon was a weather indicator.

INTRODUCTION

When someone mentions the word "Fenway" in any conversation in Boston, the first thing that automatically comes into most people's minds is Fenway Park and the world-famous Boston Red Sox. The park dominates the Fenway of Boston in both attitude and actual space, but it is only one segment of the Fenway's rich history, which includes the Olmstead-designed Muddy River and Fens, referred to as the Emerald Necklace, with the river edged with serpentine paths and foliage that creates an arboretum. By the beginning of the 20th century, the Fenway, which was often referred to as the Back Bay Fens in the area of Governor's Square (until 1932, when it was renamed Kenmore Square), had attracted such wealthy Brahmins as Isabella Stewart Gardner, the widow of financier John Lowell Gardner. Between 1900 and 1902, Isabella Stewart Gardner built a fantastic Italian palazzo with period European details that created not just a uniquely sumptuous home but an appropriate setting for her world-class museum with old masters and contemporary art that is still enjoyed decades after her death. The Fenway, due to its open lands that had only recently been infilled, also attracted numerous hospitals that were able to build large buildings and impressive campuses that could not even be considered in the older parts of the city. Among the new hospitals were the Harvard School of Medicine, the Children's Hospital, the Forsyth Dental Clinic, the New England Deaconess Hospital, and Beth Israel Hospital.

Boston's Fenway was also to become home to the city's premier cultural organizations, such as the Boston Symphony Orchestra, the Boston Opera Company, the Massachusetts Horticultural Society, the Museum of Fine Arts, and the New England Conservatory of Music. It also featured numerous places of higher education, such as the Harvard Medical School, the New England School of Pharmacy, Northeastern University, Emmanuel College, Simmons College, and Wheelock College. Most of these institutions and schools relocated or chose to build in the area of the Back Bay Fens because of large amounts of open land, much of which had been infilled in the years around the turn of the century. The neighborhood is also home to the Citgo gas sign, which sits atop the Boston University Bookstore (formerly the Peerless Motor Car building). The large neon advertising sign, 60 feet square, is triangular in design with two miles of blue and red neon tubing that illuminates Kenmore Square in the evening and acts as a prominent backdrop to Fenway Park. The sign was saved by a determined group of preservationists when it was restored in 1983, and it is now a prominent feature of the Fenway.

Today, however, Boston's Fenway is still the tree-lined neighborhood with a large park known as the Fens, which had been transformed in the late 19th century from "Muddy River" by Frederick Law Olmstead. With the Emerald Necklace, which extends from the Boston Common and Public Garden to the jewel in the necklace, Franklin Park, this green belt has been maintained for over a century and still creates an important aspect of the neighborhood and its development. Over a century later, the same bucolic setting that attracted residents and institutions in its early years still holds the same fascination today.

This history, which touches upon a section of the city of Boston that was developed only in the late 19th century, has a rich and varied history, but, as it was said in *Alice in Wonderland*, let us "begin at the beginning . . . and go on till you come to the end: then stop." Well, we will not stop, but we will continue to delve into the history and development of Boston's Fenway and the many neighborhoods of Boston.

John F. Fitzgerald, mayor of Boston, throws out the first ball at Fenway Park during a game in the 1912 World Series. Affectionately called "Honey Fitz," the mayor was accompanied by his wife, Josephine Hannan Fitzgerald (seen to the right of Fitzgerald), and their eldest daughter, Rose Fitzgerald, who in 1914 became the wife of Joseph P. Kennedy, Esq., and was the mother of John Fitzgerald Kennedy, future president of the United States. John F. Fitzgerald campaigned for the position of mayor against James Jackson Storrow (a wealthy Brahmin for whom Storrow Drive was named), using the slogan "Manhood Against Money" and "a bigger, better, busier Boston." His eternal and mellifluous renditions of "Sweet Adeline" earned him the nickname "Honey Fitz."

One

THE EARLY FENWAY

In his 1895 booklet *The Boston Park Guide*, conservationist Sylvester Baxter said that the Fenway area "is primarily an engineering work designed to effect a drainage and sanitary improvement." Baxter went on to say that "the filling of the flats remedied the danger to health to give the desirable landscape aspect to the scene, a strikingly original but beautiful simple design was adopted, in simulation of the characteristic salt-marsh scenery of the New England coast—a brackish creek, meandering amidst fens with bosky banks."

The aspect of these "bosky banks" meant that bridges in the Fenway were not just a necessity built to cross the Muddy River but were important statements of an architect's design and how it impacted the landscape. H.H. Richardson, a friend of Frederick Law Olmstead, designed his bridges in natural materials, "which led him to favor rugged textures and polychromy. The general demeanor of his work . . . stands foresquare, strong, and masculine." Following Richardson, who worked in conjunction with Olmstead in the bridge designs, the bridges of McKim, Mead & White were more classically inspired, with balustrades creating classical demarcations between the road and the edge. The architecture of these three men—Charles McKim, W.R. Mead, and Stanford White—was a major "influence on American architecture [that] was totally different from Richardson's, and it was far more pervasive."

By the beginning of the 20th century, Boston's Fenway had an exceptional charm and originality of landscape design that it attracted the attention of prospective residents and institutions and became famous as an integral part of the Emerald Necklace. Some of the areas along the Muddy River had "inlets where the [Fenway Community] gardens are now." These inlets were filled with goldfish of all sizes, and the riverbanks were dotted with ducks. The Fenway, the most elegant street in the area, was lined with impressive neo-Georgian townhouses between Boylston Street and Westland Avenue and was on a par with Boston's Back Bay.

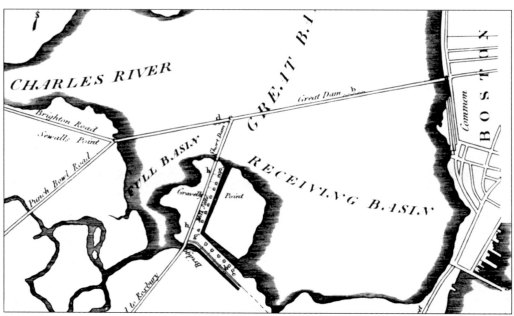

Entitled *A Survey of Boston and Its Vicinity,* this map of the Charles River and the Receiving Basin was drawn by John G. Hales in 1821 and shows the area between Boston, on the far right, and Brookline, on the left. The "Great Dam" is the present Beacon Street, and the "Road to Roxbury" is Parker Street. Boston's Fenway was created from the marshlands between Gravelly Point and Brookline.

This view looks west from the dome of the Massachusetts State House in 1857, just before the work of filling the Back Bay had begun. Beacon Street, the former "Great Dam," can be seen in the center, extending from Charles Street to Sewell's Point in Brookline. On the left is the Back Bay of Boston, a marshland that was to be infilled through John Souther and his famous steam shovel. The area of the Fenway can be seen in the distance with the two small buildings to the left of Beacon Street. In the foreground is Arlington Street, which is bordered by trees adjacent to the shoreline.

10

Looking southwest from the dome of the Massachusetts State House in 1857, this view shows the Boston Common and Public Garden in the foreground. The railroad beds of the Boston & Providence and Boston & Worcester Railroads can be seen in the distance, extending through the area of Boston's Fenway. The railroad bed eventually became Huntington Avenue, or Route 9, which is today a major roadway in the city.

This 1878 view of the Back Bay Fens from the Mission Church on Tremont Street shows the area being infilled for future development. In the foreground is the brick factory of McCormick's Brewery, one of a number of breweries that used the water of Stoney Brook for their beers and ales. The small wood houses are indicative of the working-class houses of the factory workers who created a densely built neighborhood in the mid-19th century.

William H. Whitney was a noted civil engineer who drew plans for the infilling of the Back Bay Fens. A graduate of the Lawrence Scientific School, he had served as an engineer since 1861 and was previously active in the infilling of Boston's Back Bay with Garbett & Wood. Whitney's office was at 15 Court Square, and he worked with A.S.N. Estes, a consulting engineer, in the reclamation of the marshlands.

View of Gravelly Point in 1871, drawn by civil engineer William H. Whitney, depicts an area of the tidelands and marshland of the Back Bay Fens. The drawing shows small wood-frame buildings on what became Huntington Avenue, the site of the Massachusetts Charitable Mechanics Fair Building and now the site of the Prudential Center.

The Gravelly Point area of the Back Bay Fens is depicted in this 1881 painting by Darius Cobb. The painting, entitled *Site of Boston Medical Library*, shows a cluster of small wood houses and mills on a spit of land, with the railroad tracks of the Boston & Providence Railroad in the foreground. The area was later to be the site of the Boston Medical Library, which moved from Hamilton Place across from the Park Street Church to the Fenway in 1891.

This view, looking east, was drawn by artist John Warner Barber in 1840. By that time, the Boston & Providence and Boston & Worcester Railroads had created embankments for their tracks in the marshland of Boston's Back Bay. The train in the drawing crosses the area as it approaches its depot at Park Square from about where West Newton Street is today. The dome of the Massachusetts State House surmounts Beacon Hill, and the spires of the Park Street Church and the Old South Meeting House can be seen on the right.

Frederick Law Olmstead (1822–1903) was a noted landscape architect who transformed the Muddy River into the Back Bay Fens and the Fenway of Boston. He is best known as the designer of Central Park in New York and Boston's Franklin Park, but his skills as a landscape designer earned him numerous smaller commissions and great success. Olmstead was to design Boston's park system and improve the Muddy River with a winding stream, which had banks that were planted to avoid erosion.

The Riverway, seen in 1882, had been created as a winding path of water with sloping banks on either side that were planted with grasses and reeds that would not just prevent erosion but stabilize the drainage in underground culverts.

The Riverway, seen in the early 20th century, had evolved as Olmstead had envisioned it, with wooded slopes with lawns and banks and forest-covered hills—an area that was inviting and pastoral but within walking distance of the Massachusetts State House.

John Charles Olmstead (1852–1920) was the stepson of Frederick Law Olmstead and head of the Olmstead Brothers, Landscape Architects, in which he was a partner with Frederick Law Olmstead Jr. (1870–1957). The Olmstead Associates, which also included Henry Sargent Codman after 1893 and Charles Eliot after 1897, designed a Brookline Hill subdivision (1884–1892) as well as continuing the Back Bay Fens improvements. These men continued Olmstead's vision well into the 20th century.

The Riverway, seen in a view looking toward Brookline, had become a dense green belt on either side of the former Muddy River, with automobile roads following the curvilinear turns of the river. The roads, laid out for a much smaller volume of traffic, are today often overburdened by automobiles during rush-hour traffic.

A man rows his boat in 1895 on the easterly cove of the Muddy River in the Fenway. One observer, James McKenzie, described this area of the Fenway in 1895 as "all marsh and fens and wild shrubbery. I used to see pheasants going across the road to the field." The bucolic and almost country-like atmosphere is still evident in certain areas, especially in the early-morning hours, when automobile traffic is slow, or even nonexistent.

The Agassiz Bridge in the Fens was built in 1888 of stones and arches supporting a road over the Muddy River. Here, in 1910, the bridge was covered in shrubbery and bushes, softening the effect of the rough stones.

The Agassiz Bridge was named for Jean Louis Rodolphe Louis Agassiz (1807–1873), a native of Friborg, Switzerland, and a prominent naturalist who was professor of zoology at Harvard College from 1848 to 1873. Agassiz and his well-educated family made a lasting impression on Cambridge. His second wife, Ida Higginson Agassiz, was the founder of Radcliffe College.

The Boylston Street Bridge in the Fens was designed by H.H. Richardson and, although it served the purpose of providing passage over the Muddy River, it was built of fieldstone with gently undulating buttresses on either side of the arch. It is decidedly foresquare and strong. The verticality of the Lombardy poplar trees makes for an interesting juxtaposition with the horizontality of the bridge.

This bucolic scene in the Fens shows a stone bridge, with its supporting arches, crossing the Muddy River. With trees on the banks of the river and dense greenery, it is easy to see why the appellation "Boston's Emerald Necklace" was given to this area.

The western entrance to the Fenway from the junction of Hemenway Street and Westland Avenue was marked by two white-marble piers and a fountain that were placed there in memory of Jesse C. Johnson by his widow, Ellen C. Johnson, the former superintendent of the Reformatory for Women at Sherborn, Massachusetts. A mounted policeman pauses for the photographer between the piers, and the rear of the townhouses on the Fenway can be seen in the distance.

A statue of Lief Eriksson—or "the Lucky," as he was known to his contemporaries on account of his rescuing a shipwrecked crew—was the discoverer of Vinland, an area somewhere between Portsmouth and Cape Cod. His bronze statue, sculpted in 1886 by Anne Whitney with a stern visage looking to the setting sun in the west over the Charles River, was placed on the Commonwealth Avenue Mall at Charlesgate East after the suggestion of Ole Bull and through a fundraising effort by Thomas Gold Appleton.

The former Muddy River had become the more fashionable Back Bay Fens by the beginning of the 20th century, with Commonwealth Avenue and the center mall extending through this area to Governor's (now Kenmore) Square. The streets on either side of the Muddy River were Charlesgate East and Charlesgate West, and they were the entrance to the Back Bay Fens. Frederick Law Olmstead had created this entrance to the Fens as a classically inspired area with balustrades and stone walls to the more rustic setting of the Fenway. On the right can be seen the Hotel Somerset, and on the left are the impressive townhouses on Commonwealth Avenue between Charlesgate East and Massachusetts Avenue.

The Somerset Hotel, which was designed by Arthur Bowditch and built in 1895 at the corner of Commonwealth Avenue and Charlesgate East, was a six-story hotel built on the edge of the Back Bay Fens. Horse-drawn carriages pull up in front of the fashionable hotel c. 1905. Today, the once fashionable hotel has been converted to luxury condominiums.

Commonwealth Avenue, seen from Charlesgate West, was designed by Frederick Law Olmstead as the overpass to the Muddy River, which he subjugated to the design with classical balustrades and open lawns. In the distance can be seen Governor's (later Kenmore) Square, the junction of Commonwealth and Brookline Avenues and Beacon Street.

Charlesgate East ran along the eastern side of the Muddy River and was part of the Back Bay development of the 19th-century infilling project. Pictured in a view looking toward Beacon Street, the Charlesgate Apartments overlooked the Muddy River with a steep roof with dormers and turrets. Behind the trees in the foreground is a monument to Patrick A. Collins (1844–1905), the mayor of Boston from 1902 to 1905. Sculpted by Henry Hudson Kitson and his wife, Theo Alice Ruggles Kitson, it had a bronze bust on a high pedestal, which was mourned by the figures Columbia and Erin. The monument was moved in 1969 to the mall between Clarendon and Dartmouth Streets.

Commonwealth Avenue, seen in a view from a window in the Hotel Somerset, was continued from the mall starting at Arlington Street opposite the Public Garden to Governor's Square. The alley of trees, four abreast, created an impressive march of greenery that was flanked on either side by townhouses and hotels. In the distance, on the left, can be seen Temple Adath Israel, which moved from Boston's South End to Commonwealth Avenue.

A bronze monument to John Boyle O'Reilly (1844–1890) was sculpted by Daniel Chester French and was erected in 1896 at the Boylston Street entrance to the Fenway with the inscription "Poet, Patriot, Orator." The monument was a double one, with a bronze bust in front of a Celtic design and the other of Erin supported by the figures of her sons Courage and Poetry. A member of the Fenian movement, O'Reilly was banished to Australia but jumped ship before arriving there, being taken on board the *Gazelle*. He was later to be transferred to the *Sapphire*, which brought him to America in 1869, after which he became editor of the *Pilot*, the leading Catholic newspaper in Boston. He was a successful lecturer, writer, and poet. His best-known poems were "The Pilgrim Fathers" and "Mayflower."

The Second Church in Boston was designed by Ralph Adams Cram (1863–1942) and was built at Audubon Circle, the dividing line between Boston and Brookline in the Fenway. Built with a refined design in the English Georgian style, the church had moved from Boylston Street between Dartmouth and Clarendon Street to the Fenway in 1913 due to commercial encroachment. The church, which was once known as the Old North Church and founded in 1649, was the second church to be founded in Boston, and this represented its seventh edifice. Today, the Second Church has merged with the First Church in Boston, and this edifice is used by the Ruggles Baptist Church as its place of worship.

The Speedway in the Back Bay Fens was known as the Fenway, a curvilinear motor road that encircled the former Muddy River. Here, two early automobiles head west on the road, with the dome of the First Church of Christ, Scientist seen in the distance.

The Fenway, seen from the west, was designed by Frederick Law Olmstead as an area that like the Back Bay was reclaimed from marshlands and became prominent in the westward expansion of the city. Many imposing institutions, residences, and hospitals relocated here at the beginning of the 20th century and created a distinctly urban area.

Two

THE GARDNER MUSEUM

The Gardner Museum in Boston's Fenway is an expression of the genius of its founder, Isabella Stewart Gardner, the widow of John Lowell Gardner. Fenway Court, as it has been known to Bostonians for over a century, was built of architectural fragments and details imported from Italy and assembled in a way to re-create an Italian palace of the Renaissance and provide the appropriate setting for Isabella Stewart Gardner's fabled collection of old master paintings, tapestries, sculptures, and contemporary works of art. It has been said that there "is probably no other collection in the world of similar size and diversity, gathered by an individual, which exhibits such exceptional excellence." The museum was incorporated in 1900, and its construction was completed two years later. The grand opening of the Gardner Museum was held on January 1, 1903, following a concert by 50 members of the Boston Symphony Orchestra in the music room. The honored guests marveled at the Venetian palace and its glorious courtyard, which was lighted by burning torchères and the garden in full bloom.

Exceptional excellence is probably an understatement, for Isabella Stewart Gardner's collection was unrivaled even in her lifetime and included such contemporary works as *El Jaleo* and *Portrait of Mrs. Gardner*, by John Singer Sargent; *Portrait of the Artist's Mother*, by James Whistler; and *The Omnibus*, by Zorn. However, the assemblage of old masters were headed by *Rape of Europa*, by Titian; *The Head of Christ*, by Giorgione; *Death and Assumption of the Virgin*, by Fra Angelico; and *Self Portrait, Storm at Sea*, and *A Burgomaster and His Wife*, by Rembrant. These and many other works were acquired by a woman whose motto was *C'est Mon Plaisir* (It's My Pleasure). She even had it carved into the lintel above the front entrance to her home. Today, the Gardner Museum, a "museum for the education and enjoyment of the public forever," attracts art lovers from around the world who marvel not just at the impressive collection of old masters but at the display in the Venetian palace created by a visionary a century ago in Boston's Fenway.

"It's my pleasure" may have been Isabella Stewart Gardner's response to her museum, but today, it is our pleasure.

Fenway Court, seen in a photograph from 1910, was designed by Boston architect Willard T. Sears (1837–1920) and was built at 280 The Fenway, facing an inlet of water designed by Frederick Law Olmstead as part of the Emerald Necklace. At the request of John Lowell Gardner, Sears made preliminary designs for the building in 1898, which was to be at the corner of the Fenway and Worthington Road. The design was to incorporate architectural details and fragments brought from Europe.

Isabella Stewart Gardner (1840–1924) was the wife of Boston financier John Lowell Gardner. The Gardners were sophisticated world travelers and had amassed an impressive art collection, which was displayed in their Back Bay townhouse, 152 Beacon Street. The Gardners had discussed building a museum for their collection and had architectural drawings prepared, but Mr. Gardner's death in 1898 halted the idea for a short period of time. Mrs. Gardner, however, took their idea and, with Willard T. Sears, her architect, created a personal fantasy that has often be referred to as the best small art museum in the world.

The setting of Fenway Court gives, in some ways, the impression of an Italian villa set in the countryside. It is not surprising that Fenway Court looked like an Italian palazzo with the purchase in Venice of "columns, capitals, reliefs, frescoes, glass, mirrors, cassoni, chairs, fountains, balconies, and 'facciate di palazzo.'" Reeds and grasses of the banks create a naturalistic landscape for the house, which still creates quite an impression as one comes across it in the Fenway.

The side of the Gardner Museum facing Evans Way (formerly Worthington Road) had a high wall enclosing the Monk's Garden, with a series of Moorish-inspired arches projecting above the wall. Isabella Stewart Gardner's personal living quarters were on the fourth floor of Fenway Court. A balcony can be seen just below the overhanging tile roof.

In this view from the cloister, the courtyard is framed by two colonettes resting on stone lions that flank the archway leading to the most beautiful place in Boston during the winter months. The opening of Fenway Court on January 1, 1903, followed a concert by the Boston Symphony Orchestra in the music room. After the concert, the mirrored wall shielding the courtyard was rolled back, and the assembled guests must have looked through to the courtyard in astonishment at the scene of a glorious garden in the middle of a Boston winter.

The courtyard at Fenway Court has a tile pavement purchased by the Gardners in Rome and installed as the central feature of the courtyard. The terrazzo-tile pavement, surrounded by pieces of antiquity, acts as a visual focal point in the courtyard, which had plants and blooming flowers throughout the year.

A corner of the courtyard shows the assemblage of architectural details that were purchased by Isabella Stewart Gardner in Europe and were incorporated into her new Venetian palace in Boston's Fenway. Willard T. Sears may have been the architect of Fenway Court, but Isabella Stewart Gardner was the creator. Her vision was not just for effect but for a sense of permanence for her collection. Fenway Court is ageless, and it will be not just a monument to its creator but a temple where art worshipers can gather to appreciate the Gardner collection in a sumptuous and invigorating atmosphere.

The cloister at Fenway Court encircled the courtyard. Here, two stone lions—one roaring over a victim, holding him down with his paw—act as bases to colonettes that support a brick arcade.

The music room, pictured in 1904, was a large white room with a horseshoe staircase at one end and the performance stage at the other. On the opening night of Fenway Court, January 1, 1903, Isabella Stewart Gardner stood at the top of this staircase in a black gown with her diamond antennae waving above her head to receive her guests and to welcome her friends and fellow Brahmins to her new home and to a concert by 50 members of the Boston Symphony Orchestra. In 1914, the music room was divided in two lengthwise; the upper portion became the tapestry room, and the lower portion became the Spanish cloister, with its fabled John Singer Sargent painting *El Jaleo*.

The tapestry room was designed to display the fabulous Ffoulke-Barberini tapestries that Isabella Stewart Gardner had acquired on her trips to Europe. The "Chateau and Garden" tapestries were acquired from the Charles M. Ffoulke collection. "Archduke Albert and Archduchess Isabella," "Abraham and Rebecca," and "Boy in Tree and other Springtime Illustrations," all of which had previously been in the Barberini collection in Rome, were from Mrs. Ffoulke. After its completion in 1926, Gardner used the tapestry room to receive guests on Sunday afternoons and to serve them tea from a refractory table. Today, the tapestry room is where the concerts are held.

The Dutch room at Fenway Court was, with the chapel, the only room to be closed to guests on the opening night of Fenway Court. It remained unseen by the public until after Isabella Stewart Gardner's death. Here was placed John Singer Sargent's portrait of Mrs. Gardner, which had been unseen since its showing in 1888 at the St. Botolph Club per the direction of her husband. Today, the portrait is the major feature of the room.

The chapel at Fenway Court was said to have been built in memory of Jackie Gardner, Isabella and John Lowell Gardner's only child, who had died in 1865. The chapel was where the body of Mrs. Gardner was laid and the prayers for the dead were read before her funeral at the Church of the Advent. The chapel is furnished with oak choir stalls and is the annual setting for a memorial mass for Mrs. Gardner by priests from Beacon Hill's Church of the Advent. On either side are torchères that were purchased in Venice and once stood in the Gardners' Back Bay townhouse.

John Singer Sargent (1856–1925) depicted Isabella Stewart Gardner in a portrait painted in 1888. The painting, displayed at the St. Botolph Club, shows her to be "plain of face and beautiful of person." Mr. Gardner decreed that the portrait should never be exhibited during his lifetime, and it remained unviewed until after Mrs. Gardner's death. It is today displayed in the Gothic Room above a long carved-oak coffer that has vases of madonna lillies at the base of the portrait. Mrs. Gardner may have, as her will states, intended that Fenway Court be "a museum for the education and enjoyment of the public forever," but a stipulation decrees that nothing may be moved and "should be left forever exactly as she left it" or the collection is to be sold to benefit Harvard University.

Isabella Stewart Gardner is seen holding a large leather volume that was bound by Mary C. Sears and given to her by friends who lauded her for her untiring work in the creation of Fenway Court. Gardner still proves an enigma to many Bostonians and those who visit Fenway Court, as so much has been written about her that is conjecture rather than fact. Henry Adams, the great historian and scion of the prominent Adams family once said to Gardner, "You are a creator, and stand alone." However, she has become part of Boston lore as having walked a lion on Boylston Street, washing the steps of the Church of the Advent to atone for her sins, and hiring two burly boxers for a match in her parlor with her female friends in attendance.

Three

THE MUSEUM
OF FINE ARTS

Established in 1870, the Museum of Fine Arts is one of the great art museums of the world. The museum was originally located at the corner of St. James and Dartmouth Streets in a Ruskinian Gothic building designed by Sturgis & Brigham and built in 1876 facing Art Square, or what was renamed Copley Square in 1883. A Victorian red-brick building with a number of high-style architectural details, it was enlarged over the next three decades but proved wholly insufficient in space and exhibit space so that trustees voted to move to Boston's Fenway, where numerous institutions and schools had been moving since the turn of the century. In 1907, ground was broken on a large tract of land facing Huntington Avenue between Museum Road, The Fenway, and Greenleaf Street.

The new museum was designed by noted architect Guy Lowell, who was assisted by architects R. Clipston Sturgis, Edmund March Wheelwright, and D. Despradelle, and it was built in 1908–1909 in a severely classic design with a center pavilion with four Ionic columns flanked by symmetrical wings. The museum was further enlarged with the Evans Memorial Wing, also designed by Guy Lowell and built in 1911–1915, as a colonnade of Ionic columns facing the Fenway. Throughout the 20th century, the museum acquired by gift and purchase many notable pieces of art and is today considered among the world's great art museums. A new wing known as the Decorative Arts Wing was built in 1924–1928. The west wing was designed by I.M. Pei Associates and completed in 1981 as a stone-clad, glass-topped wing that, although adjacent to Lowell's more classical design, does not intrude nor assert itself in the overall design. Today, a new wing is being built for the American Decorative Arts, which is being designed by Foster and Partners, London.

The Huntington Avenue facade of the Museum of Fine Arts has a center pavilion with flanking wings. It was said at the time of its completion that this "new palace is a monumental and imposing structure, a signal architectural triumph, and a perfect expression of the modern museum of art." Founded in 1870, the first museum was opened in 1876 on the site of the Copley Plaza Hotel in Copley Square. By 1908, however, ground had been broken for the present museum, which opened a year later in Boston's Fenway.

Guy Lowell (1870–1927) was the architect of the Boston Museum of Fine Arts. This pencil sketch of the architect was done by John Singer Sargent in the museum. Lowell continued to design additions to the museum, including the Evans Memorial Wing in 1915 and the Decorative Arts Wing and Garden (1928). Lowell also designed the School of the Museum of Fine Arts, which was opened in 1927 and, in 1987, was expanded and renovated by Graham Gund Architects.

The museum wings are nearly complete in 1909 as the A.B. Stannard Company works to complete the center pavilion.

The east wing of the museum is under construction in 1908. The two horses in the foreground pull a sledge with stone for the building, which has staging on the partially completed second floor.

Workers had applied copperwork and skylights to the roof of the museum by the fall of 1908. During its construction, there were 25,000 square feet of skylights and 60,000 square feet of copper roofing. This work was done by E. Van Noorden Company, which was established in 1873 and located on Massachusetts Avenue in Boston.

The temple-fronted center pavilion of the Museum of Fine Arts has Ionic columns supporting a pediment with a rusticated base. The severity of the classical design is offset by the tall windows that punctuate the facade and the Ionic columns that project from the front of the museum. The design seems perfect for what has become a world-class museum. As one enters by the Huntington Avenue doors, the rotunda at the top of the staircase has ceiling murals by John Singer Sargent (1856–1925), completed in 1921.

Appeal to the Great Spirit was sculpted by Cyrus Edwin Dallin (1861–1944) and placed on the forecourt of the Huntington Avenue entrance to the museum. A moving bronze statue of a Native American astride his horse, it is the quintessential memorial to those who lived in Massachusetts Bay Colony before the Puritans arrived in 1630.

Kuan-Yin, the Divinity of Compassion is a 12th-century sculpture of Chinese art at the Museum of Fine Arts. The collection of asiatic art in the museum is comprehensive and among the finest in this country, and much of it was donated to the museum by Bostonians, including Edward Jackson Holmes and John Gardner Coolidge of Boston's Back Bay.

The Japanese Garden at the Museum of Fine Arts was designed to replicate a courtyard of a residence in old Japan. Here, with a small garden with pathways crossing over pools of water, a large pagoda and other typical garden ornaments embellish the installation.

The garden courtyard at the Museum of Fine Arts had formal gardens surrounding a large circular playing fountain in the center. The evergreen trees came from Boxford and, when planted, gave an attractive area for museum visitors to rest. Designed by noted landscape architect Arthur A. Shurtleff, in collaboration with Henry Forbes Bigelow, William T. Aldrich, and Edwin H. Holmes, a pleasant and inviting area was created.

The west wing of the Museum of Fine Arts had large flowering shrubs along the foundation with classical statuary set on plinth bases along the Huntington Avenue facade. Eventually, the Decorative Arts Wing and Garden, which was designed by Guy Lowell and opened in November 1928, would be expanded by the west wing, a modern addition designed by I.M. Pei and opened in July 1981.

One of the sculptures in front of the museum was a bronze statue of Nathaniel Hawthorne (1804–1864), by noted sculptor Bela Pratt. Hawthorne is among the best-known authors in this country, and among his bestselling books are *The Scarlet Letter* (1850), *The Snow-Image and Other Twice Told Tales* (1852), and *Mosses from an Old Manse* (1846). A prolific and insightful author, he often wrote using old New England themes that were concerned with the ethical problems of sin, punishment, and atonement.

The garden courtyard was designed by the noted landscape architect Arthur Asahel Shurtleff (1870–1957), who worked with the director of the museum and a committee of architects to create a visually inviting area. In the center was a large capital that served as a water well with a cast-iron framework from which a water bucket was suspended. The wood boxes that hold evergreen balls are very attractive, and all of the features combine for a relaxing garden.

The terracing at the courtyard had bold, squat balusters forming a balustrade that encircled the open area. With the placement of statuary at the end of a vista, the garden had a formality that was impressive yet inviting. Today, the area is known as the Fraser Garden Court Terrace. It was redesigned by Jung Brannen Associates and opened in December 1998.

Seen from across the Fenway, the Evans Memorial Wing presents a classically elegant facade for the museum. Built of granite with a colonnade of Ionic columns, decorative inset panels, and a low hip roof, Lowell's addition makes a bold statement. The museum has long been said to embody "the results of studies of the principle museums of Europe and of modern museology, made by advisory committees composed of artists and architects, in connection with the director and museum staff." The lagoon in the foreground was created in 1927, when the area was graded and prepared for landscaping.

Robert Dawson Evans (1843–1909) and his wife, Maria Antoinette Hunt Evans (1845–1917), were not only the benefactors of the Evans Memorial Wing of the Museum of Fine Arts but also generous donors of a large collection of paintings. Designed by Guy Lowell, the wing has a colonnade of Ionic columns flanked by bay projections. It has presented an impressive facade facing the Fenway since its opening in February 1915. A native of Canada, Evans lived in Boston's Back Bay on Commonwealth Avenue and was principal of the United States Rubber Company.

The rose garden in the Fenway acts as an elegant forecourt to the Evans Memorial Wing of the Museum of Fine Arts. The garden was designed by noted landscape architect Arthur A. Shurcliff in the early 20th century with hundreds of rose bushes planted in a formal garden plan. The garden's rose bushes, hedges, arbors, and standard roses attracted many admirers during the blooming season. Today, the garden is being planted with a dramatic increase in the number and variety of roses, which will lengthen the blooming season. On the right can be seen the lagoon near the Fenway, and near here is a Japanese temple bell cast in 1675. The bell was taken from Manpukuji Temple-Sendai by a group of soldiers from the USS *Boston* at the end of World War II. Given by the mayor of Kyoto to the citizens of Boston as a token of peace and friendship, it was placed near the rose garden.

The Kelleher Rose Garden, named in 1975 for James P. Kelleher and said to be "one of the most beautiful and best-kept secrets in the Emerald Necklace," is currently undergoing a restoration by the city parks department, in cooperation with the Emerald Necklace Conservancy, to re-create the original plans of Arthur Shurtleff, who also designed the garden courtyard at the Museum of Fine Arts. It has been said that the conservancy has convened "a dedicated group of rosarians, landscape architects, horticultural specialists and garden club representatives to develop a Master Plan for The Rose Garden's renewal in order to bring beauty back to a once spectacular rose garden."

Four

SYMPHONY HALL AND THE OPERA HOUSE

Boston is music, and music is Boston. The Boston Symphony Orchestra was founded in 1881 by Henry Lee Higginson, a man known as Boston's First Citizen, and first performed in the Boston Music Hall (now the Orpheum Theatre) on Hamilton Place in downtown Boston. It was "Mr. Gericke who really made the orchestra, forming it from an engaging band of clever musicians, but undisciplined, into the perfect organization working in harmony under the one leader." For the next two decades, the orchestra continued to perform, but the hall soon proved inadequate, and funds were raised to construct a hall specifically designed for concerts. Charles McKim of the nationally known architectural firm of McKim, Mead & White created an acoustically perfect hall, thanks to Prof. Wallace C. Sabine of Harvard University, that was widely accepted by the public. Boston's taste for opera had been piqued by troops who toured Boston, but it was in 1908 that Eben Dyer Jordan, proprietor of the great Jordan Marsh & Company department store, founded the opera.

The Boston Opera House was a success for its first decade, but it was sold by Eben Jordan in 1916. By 1920, "the Opera House was empty most of the year, as there were few opportunities for opera to be enjoyed on a regular and sustained basis in the city." Sometimes, a big show from New York would use it, and annually the Metropolitan Opera would claim it for a week, but the majority of the time, the elegant hall remained silent and empty. Occasionally, the New York City Opera came on tour and played there, but it was to languish until its unfortunate demolition in 1958. The Boston Symphony Orchestra, however, proved not just an immediate success in its new location, but it continually sustained its patronage by Bostonians of all walks of life.

The cornerstone of the Boston Opera House was laid on December 1, 1908, by Eben Dyer Jordan, with Gov. Curtis Guild presenting an address to the large audience. Designed by Wheenwright & Haven and built by the George W. Harvey Company, the opera house was a series of galleries, circles, boxes, and elegant spaces that catered to those who loved the opera or thought it the place to be seen on opening night. The Boston Opera House was said to be "a manifestation of the architectural renaissance for which, no less than for one's awakenings of the mind and spirit, the present age will be distinguished."

Eben Dyer Jordan (1857–1916) was the benefactor of the Boston Opera House and was the man for whom Jordan Hall of the New England Conservatory of Music was named. A co-owner of Jordan Marsh & Company, a leading department store in New England founded by his father and Ephriam Marsh, he was a generous benefactor to the arts in Boston.

The Boston Opera House, said to have a "simple, dignified facade," was designed by Parkman B. Haven of the Boston architectural firm of Wheelwright & Haven and built of red-brick and white terra-cotta facings in 1908–1909. The operas were subscribed to by not just opera lovers but also by Boston's social elite who patronized its gala opening evening performances. The facade had four monumental engaged Ionic columns supporting a pediment with projecting piers on either side that were for the staircases. Under the main cornice and recesses were emblematical statuary bas-reliefs by the noted sculptor Bela Pratt.

Parkman B. Haven of the Boston architectural firm of Wheelwright & Haven was the architect of the Boston Opera House. With Prof. Wallace C. Sabine, study had been undertaken on the acoustical problems, which were corrected, and the opera house became "a perfect building for seeing and hearing." In his 1915 book *Boston Today*, noted historian Edwin Bacon said that the Boston Opera House was "one of the best arranged and constructed theatre buildings in the new world."

45

The proscenium of the Boston Opera House was ornamented in the Italian Renaissance style and had a large velvet curtain, which was provided by Jordan Marsh Company. When opened, the curtain often revealed magnificently painted stage sets that accompanied the operas. The house could seat 2,750 people, and the house had 84 boxes arranged in two grand tiers and in triplicate bays on either side of the proscenium with a mahogany door to each box with the owners' names on them. There was also first circle, second circle, and standing room for the true opera afficionados who often could not afford tickets.

Henry Russell was the director of the Boston Opera Company. A successful and dynamic man, he had the full confidence of Eben Dyer Jordan. In the first decade of the Boston Opera Company's existence, Russell made it one of the best known in the country.

Members of the Boston Opera Company in 1909 included such renowned artists as, from left to right, the following: (first row) C. Urban, B. Lombardi, and Gualtiero Fabi; (second row) O. Spirescu, Antonio Muschietto, and Raymond Roze; (third row) O. Sbavaglia, A. Luzzatti, and Ralph Lyford; (fourth row) Mesdames Muschietto and Maria Paporello.

Symphony Hall, which is at the corner of Huntington and Massachusetts Avenues, is the home of the Boston Symphony Orchestra. Designed in a modified Renaissance style by the noted architectural firm of McKim, Mead & White, the "Temple of Music" was dedicated in 1900. With its relocation from the old Boston Music Hall (now known as the Orpheum Theatre) on Hamilton Place in downtown Boston, it set the tone for many of the impressive buildings erected in the Fenway during the first two decades of the 20th century. The orchestra was led by Wilhelm Gericke, who served as conductor from 1898 to 1906.

Maj. Henry Lee Higginson (1834–1919) was a wealthy banker in Boston who "founded the Symphony Orchestra in Boston as a gift to the community." Known as Boston's First Citizen, he was a well-respected man and developer who built the Agassiz, a Commonwealth Avenue apartment house that he named for his wife. Higginson said in 1900 that the orchestra "has done our city and our country signal and intelligent service such as ennobles and educates a nation."

The interior of Symphony Hall, seen in 1904, is still considered Boston's "Temple of Music," with only the name Beethoven to be seen in letters above the stage. The successor to the old Boston Music Hall, the hall is where the concerts of the Boston Symphony Orchestra and the oratorios of the Handel and Haydn Society are given as well as the popular summer Pops concerts. The Pops are popular concerts "by a part of the orchestra, of airy music, running through the early summer months, with a mild dash of bohemianism, the audience sitting about little tables at which light drinks and lighter edibles are served. [It has] become a unique Boston institution."

A crowd waits in front of the Huntington Avenue colonnade for the sale of Friday afternoon "rush seats," which were reduced-priced unsold tickets offered just before the beginning of the concert, with many people arriving on Friday morning, as they were "music lovers who couldn't afford tickets." It was once said that "Friday afternoons during the season assume the aspect of local holy days dedicated to the classics and a vast craning of necks to be certain that the Hallowells and Forbses are in their accustomed stalls."

Patrons of the Boston Symphony Orchestra begin to arrive for a concert in 1950, with the floor and second balcony seats only half filled. The plaster casts in the niches in the background were placed there after 1901 by Prof. Wallace C. Sabine (then assistant professor of physics at Harvard University) for acoustical reasons. However, the classical life-sized plaster casts also add a decorative touch to the elegant interior of Symphony Hall.

A section of the stage in January 1950 shows Charles Munch (1891–1968) conducting a Pension Fund concert of the Boston Symphony Orchestra. Munch was a native of Strasbourg, where he became a professor of the Strasbourg Conservatory before his arrival in the United States in 1946. He became conductor of the Boston Symphony Orchestra in 1949, following the 25-year career of Serge Koussevitzky (1924–1949.)

Symphony Hall, seen from the second balcony, is an acoustically perfect space that has been the home of not just the Boston Symphony Orchestra but the Handel and Haydn Society and the Boston Pops. The great organ, which has a tonal design known as "American classic," was designed by G. Donald Harrison and built by the Aeolian-Skinner Company of Boston. It was installed in the summer of 1949. The organ has 4,802 pipes and 67 stops, all adjustable at the console either by hand or by 12 general pistons controlling the entire instrument resources.

The Chorus Pro Musica, with orchestra conducted by Alfred Nash Patterson in 1950, performs Bach's B Minor Mass with the Boston Symphony Orchestra. The Chorus Pro Musica, established in 1948, is known "for innovative programming and high quality performances [and] has collaborated with such famed organizations as the Boston Symphony Orchestra, the Boston Philharmonic, the Boston Ballet," and others. Its music director is currently Jeffrey Rink.

Seiji Ozawa became the music director of the Boston Symphony Orchestra in 1973 and is the 30th conductor of the orchestra since its founding in 1881. A native of Hoten, Manchuria, he had previously served as music director of the Ravinia Festival in Illinois, music director of the Toronto Symphony, and music director and conductor of the San Francisco Symphony Orchestra, a position he held in conjunction with Boston until 1976, when he resigned and has remained in Boston since.

Five

A NEIGHBORHOOD ARISES

Boston's Fenway, after the infill was complete, was laid out as a series of areas that had streets such as Queensberry, Peterborough, Jersey, and Kilmarnock Streets and Audubon Road, all of which had picturesque names and were envisioned as being developed for Boston's growing middle class with large apartment buildings. The Fenway developed as "a quiet residential area, more like a village than a city district, in contrast to its neighbor across the park. The calm and beauty of the Fens have become an integral part of the neighborhood."

However, it was the extension of the streetcar line from the Back Bay that gave the greatest impetus for growth in the Fenway. In the 1880s, Boylston Street was extended west from Exeter Street to the new Fenway, and the basic lines of the neighborhood were drawn. Soon, numerous streetcars began to service the area, and by 1887, "they merged with the West End Street Railway Company, the first in Boston to experiment with electric transit cars. By 1892, lines ran on Huntington Avenue, Beacon Street, Massachusetts Avenue, and Boylston Street, making it possible for people to live in the Fenway and work, shop, and amuse themselves in Boston." The major connection in the Fenway is Kenmore Square, which was located in the center of Governor's (later Kenmore) Square and is today the gateway to Boston via the Green Line.

In the late 19th century, new streets—such as The Fenway, Westland Avenue, and St. Stephen, Batavia (once a notorious red-light district that was renamed Symphony Road), Hemenway (formerly Parker Street), Astor (now Burbank Street), and Gainsborough Streets—were laid out with brick houses and apartment buildings that were rapidly being built to create a new neighborhood. These buildings were invariably built of red brick and were Queen Anne inspired, sometimes with a Romanesque arch or a Victorian detail but not elaborate or architecturally significant. However, along Huntington Avenue, it was "all apartment houses, from Mass. Avenue up to Irvington Street, where they built the Massachusetts Turnpike."

The Johnson Memorial flanked the western entrance to the Fenway. Designed by Guy Lowell, it was erected in memory of Jesse C. Johnson by his widow, Ellen C. Johnson, in 1901. The twin limestone pylons and the fountain created an elegant entrance to the Fenway.

The Johnson Memorial, seen in the foreground, was located at the end of Westland Avenue. The impressive Beaux Arts apartment building on the right was designed by Guy Lowell in 1904–1905. The building later served as the Trade High School for Girls.

A motorcar has just passed though the Johnson Memorial and is traveling west on The Fenway. In the distance can be seen the Hemenway Chambers, a fashionable hotel at the corner of Hemenway Street and Westand Avenue.

The Hemenway Chambers was a six-story apartment building with a mansard roof with two stories of dormers. Designed by John Lavalle (1865–1916), it was a modern hotel centrally located with "the harmonious atmosphere of a private home." Today, the former hotel has been converted to senior housing.

The Fritz Carlton Hotel (later known as the Hotel Boylston) was designed as a high-style Beaux Arts hotel at the corner of Boylston Street and East Charlesgate. Obviously named in a lighthearted comparison to the five-star Ritz Carlton Hotel on Arlington Street in Boston's Back Bay, the Fritz Carlton was a reasonably priced alternative but was just as convenient, with the streetcar located just a block away at Massachusetts Avenue. During the early years of the 20th century, the Fenway was developed with large apartment buildings, such as the Fenmore across the street, and this hotel was not only impressive but following the trend for larger buildings rather than townhouses. The former hotel was purchased by the Berklee College of Music, which was founded in 1945 by Lawrence Berk as the Scillinger House of Music. It became known as Berklee School of Music in honor of its founder in 1954 and was renovated for administrative offices and academic departments. The school, which was accredited in 1973, is now known as the Berklee College of Music and has numerous sites throughout the Fenway for its approximate 3,400 students. Today, the college is headed by Lee Eliot Berk, son of the founder, who serves as president of the world's largest independent music college and the premier institution for the study of contemporary music.

The Hotel Somerset is located at the corner of Charlesgate East and Commonwealth Avenue adjacent to the Back Bay Fens. An impressive hotel designed by Arthur Bowditch and built in 1897, it was both fashionable and elegant, as the "decoration of the interior is rich and artistic in the extreme." Today, the former hotel has been converted into luxury condominiums.

A motorcar travels along the Fenway, one of the curvilinear motorways laid out by Frederick Law Olmstead and the Olmstead Associates at the turn of the century. One of the interesting aspects of the plantings was the use of Lombardy poplar trees to line the new motorways; the verticality of the trees gave an almost Italian countryside feeling to the Fenway and the Back Bay Fens.

The Massachusetts Horticultural Society commissioned the Boston architectural firm of Wheelwright & Haven to design its new headquarters, which was built at the corner of Massachusetts and Huntington Avenues. The hall, the third building of the society since it was founded in 1829, is probably one of the best examples of the English Baroque style of architecture in the city, with Ionic pilasters between the windows, a classical swagged cornice, and rich full-blown architectural details.

Edmund March Wheelwright (1854–1912) served as city architect for Boston from 1891 to 1894. He was a prominent architect in partnership with Parkman B. Haven in the architectural firm of Wheelwright & Haven. Wheelwright & Haven designed numerous structures in the city, among them Horticultural Hall, the New England Conservatory of Music, the Mechanic Arts High School, the Harvard Lampoon Building at Harvard University, and the Longfellow Bridge across the Charles River.

Charles Sprague Sargent (1841–1927) was appointed the first director of the Arnold Arboretum, which (although owned by Harvard University) was an important horticultural study area, with the Bussey Institute offering a degree. Sargent served for five decades and was also chair of arborculture at Harvard University and author of *The Sylva of North America*.

The library at Horticultural Hall "is the oldest and most comprehensive horticultural resource center in the world and is renowned for its collection of books related to early agriculture, horticulture, and landscape design."

Horticultural Hall was the third building of the Massachusetts Horticultural Society, which had been founded in 1829. The first building was a granite Greek Revival structure built in 1844, which was designed by Isaiah Rogers, on School Street, and the second a granite Italianate structure built in 1864, which was designed by Gridley J. Fox Bryant, on Tremont Street.

The first chrysanthemum exhibition held in the new Horticultural Hall was in 1901. Here huge displays of chrysanthemums are displayed in a winter flower show with some in large Rose Medallion Chinese export porcelain urns, as seen on either side.

An exhibition in 1912 in Horticultural Hall created a garden replete with bedding plants, a pergola with cascading plants, and garden statuary that must have dazzled Bostonians a century ago in the dead of winter when they attended the flower show. Notice the murals between the arched vaults and the fact that the bedding plants are set on a wood floor, with the exhibit lasting less than two weeks before it would be dismantled.

The Massachusetts Charitable Mechanics Association Building, often referred to as Mechanics Hall, was designed by William Gibbons Preston and built in 1881 on Huntington Avenue. The venerable mechanics association was instituted in 1795 and incorporated in 1806 as a collective representative of the numerous mechanics, or artisans, in the commonwealth, with a silver medal designed by William Mitchell presented for excellence to those who exhibited their wares. Initially, industrial exhibits were held in the great halls, but the halls were eventually rented out for sundry purposes that ranged from Bible meetings, flower and fruit shows, as well as graduations from local schools, colleges, and universities.

The auditorium of Mechanics Hall was the site on June 18, 1902, of the annual meeting of the First Church of Christ, Scientist. Here, hundreds of members sit in Mechanics Hall as Mary Baker Eddy, her practitioners, and invited guests sit on the platform seen on the upper left.

Mechanics Hall was a cavernous space that had bleacher-type seating with balconies for the well-attended events held here throughout the late 19th and early 20th centuries, including fairs, flower shows, and concerts.

The Massachusetts Charitable Mechanics Association Building, seen from West Newton Street, was a long Victorian-style red-brick and brownstone building with an octagonal turreted tower on the east end. A streetcar passes the building as it travels east on Huntington Avenue toward Copley Square *c.* 1905. Mechanics Hall was demolished in 1959, and its site was developed in the mid-1960s as the Prudential Center, with the Prudential being the first true high-rise office building in Boston's Back Bay.

Eventually, Horticultural Hall proved insufficient in available space for the annual flower show of the Massachusetts Horticultural Society. Here, in 1929, the flower show was held in Mechanics Hall on Huntington Avenue, with a garden composed of Dutch flowers flanking a center fountain and water basin. These exhibits have become increasingly realistic over the last 125 years, with attendees avidly looking forward to the premier of spring, albeit indoors.

Horticultural Hall is seen here at the corner of Massachusetts and Huntington Avenue c. 1920. On the right is Chickering Hall, which at this time was Elias M. Leow's St. James Theatre. The dome of the First Church of Christ, Scientist rises high above all of the building in this part of town.

An impressive streetscape is seen here, with Symphony Hall (far left), Horticultural Hall, and Chickering Hall creating an important cultural connection in Boston's Fenway. Charles McKim of McKim, Mead & White created an Italianate-style hall that was opened in 1900. Horticultural Hall was designed by Wheelwright & Haven as an English Baroque hall, probably the best representative example of this style in New England, and opened in 1901. Chickering Hall, an impressive five-arched-facade building with engaged Corinthian columns, served as the headquarters of the Emerson School of Oratory.

The Massachusetts Historical Society, which was founded in 1791 and is considered the oldest historical society in the United States, was designed by Edmund March Wheelwright and built in 1899 at 1154 Boylston Street at the corner of the Fenway. The society met for many years in the third floor of the central pavilion of the Tontine Crescent, designed by Charles Bulfinch and built in 1793–1795 on Franklin Street. Between 1833 and 1899, the historical society was located on Tremont Street in a granite building adjacent to the King's Chapel Burying Ground.

The council meeting room of the Massachusetts Historical Society had a large circular table where the 13-member council that governs the society met. The room was furnished with historical pieces of furniture and portraits, such as those of George Washington and Samuel Adams.

The Park Riding School, a noted equestrian riding academy in Boston's Fenway, was designed by Wheelwright & Haven and built in 1900. Notice the vast amount of open space on the left of the school, with the rear of apartment buildings on the right. Today, the Park Riding School is Jillian's Boston, a popular nightclub at 145 Ipswich Street.

The Boston Arena is located on St. Botolph Street, just west of Massachusetts Avenue, and was built in 1909. Owned by the city of Boston, it has been the scene of some of the greatest athletic events ever held in Boston. It was recently renamed the Matthews Arena for George and Hope Matthews, Mr. Matthews having served as chair of Northeastern University Board of Trustees and as a respected business leader in Boston. The various tenants of the arena have included the Northeastern Huskies (NCAA) since 1930, the Boston Bruins (NHL) from 1924 to 1928, and the Boston Celtics (NBA) from 1946 to 1955. The arena has also hosted scholastic hockey teams, and Santos' Gym in the rear has now become the Makris Varsity Club Lounge.

Jordan Hall of the New England Conservatory of Music is an elegant performance hall with classical architectural details, a panel dome, and an acoustically perfect performance stage. The New England Conservatory was designed by Wheelwright & Haven and was the gift of department store magnate Eben D. Jordan. Opened in 1903 with a seating capacity of 1,013, the fine auditorium is used for performances by conservatory students who will hopefully "launch their careers in one of the world's favorite performing spaces." Jordan Hall was restored in 1995 by Ann Beha Associates, and Kirkegaard & Associates were the acoustic engineers for the project.

Eben Dyer Jordan (1857–1916) was the person for whom Jordan Hall was named. A wealthy Bostonian, he was president of Jordan Marsh & Company, which was the largest department store in New England at the beginning of the 20th century and was later absorbed by Macy's. Jordan Hall has been said to be a place "beloved for its acoustics, intimacy, and beauty. . . . NEC's Jordan Hall has been at the center of Boston's musical life since its opening" and is a fitting memorial to this Renaissance man.

The Young Men's Christian Association (YMCA) was built in 1911–1913 on Huntington Avenue. Designed by Shepley, Rutan & Coolidge, the YMCA had among its notable features a large swimming pool, which was one of the largest and best in the country in the early 20th century and was supplied by water from an artesian well. The YMCA also offered Friday night square dancing and Saturday night ballroom dancing, and if one was not interested in dancing, there was a bowling alley.

Streetcar 5955 turns onto Boylston Street from Ipswich Street *c.* 1936. In the background is St. Clement's Church, a fine example of a granite English Gothic church. Originally built as a Universalist church for the large number of Protestant residents of the area, the church was purchased by the Roman Catholic archdiocese in 1935 after a shift in the population. It was dedicated by Cardinal O'Connell and named by him for his titular church in Rome. In 1945, Archbishop Richard Cushing designated St. Clement's as the archdiocesan eucharistic shrine, with the Franciscan Missionaries of Mary to staff it.

The Second Church of Boston was designed by Ralph Adams Cram and built in 1913 at Audubon Circle at the Boston and Brookline town line. An impressive and refined English Georgian–style church, the church moved from Boylston Street, opposite Trinity Church, as the area increasingly became commercial. The church was founded in 1649 and was first in Boston's North End, where it was known as the Old North Church (not Christ Church, currently known as such). Audubon Road was laid out by Olmstead as part of the Emerald Necklace. Except for the Robert Treat Paine House, designed by Charles A. Cummings of Cummings & Sears and built in 1899 at the corner of Audubon Road and Queensberry Street, there was no building in the area until 1915.

The Fenway Studios, designed by Parker & Thomas and built in 1905, is an important building with artists' studios on Ipswich Street with northern exposure, which is desired by artists. The Fenway Studios were the successors to the Studios on Tremont Street, between Bromfield and Winter Streets, which were considered fine artists' studios in the late 19th century. At the turn of the century, during the Arts and Crafts movement, the studios were an innovative attempt for artists' studios and living space to be combined.

The entrance to the Fenway Studios shows the influence of the Arts and Crafts movement, with an arch surmounted by wrought-iron decorative balustrades. In 1981, the Fenway Studios were sold to a resident artist's cooperative committed to maintaining the space for artists.

Temple Adath Israel, designed by Clarence H. Blackall with a Byzantine exterior and an Egyptian Revival interior, was built in 1906 on Commonwealth Avenue in the Fenway for the congregation that had recently removed from the South End. In *Boston: A Guide Book*, Adath Israel is said to be "the stateliest Hebrew church in Boston." The inscription above the entrance reads, "The Eternal Our God Is One."

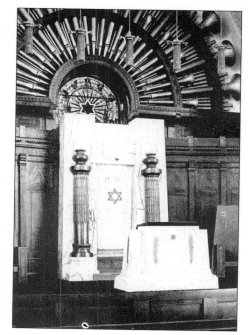

The interior of Temple Adath Israel was classical in its design, but above the bima and ark, Blackall incorporated the organ trumpets and pipes to create an impressive as well as functional design. Today, the former temple is used as Morse Auditorium of Boston University.

The Billy Sunday Tabernacle was a cavernous hutlike building located just west of Massachusetts Avenue in the Fenway. Billy Sunday was a vivacious and engaging preacher who was once offered $1 million to quit preaching a sermon on booze. Sunday's sermons were often printed verbatim in Monday newspapers, and these sermons were "preached where Catholics were forbidden to hear, but afterwards the Catholic bishops wrote the newspapers and thanked Billy Sunday for coming to their city." In the distance can be seen the Boston Opera House and the YMCA. The famed Billy Sunday Tabernacle is now part of the Northeastern University campus.

The Greek Orthodox Cathedral of New England, also known as the Church of the Evangelismos (Annunciation), was designed by architect Hachadoor S. Demoorjian, with the interior being the collaboration of three noted architects and designers: Ralph Adams Cram, Kenneth Conant, and Charles J. Connick. A Classical Revival design, the cathedral was built in 1923 between the campus of Northeastern University and Wentworth Institute of Technology. The cathedral is a Boston landmark and is listed in the National Register of Historic Places. (Courtesy of James Z. Kyprianos.)

Governor's Square, shown in a view looking east in 1915, had been created from the marshlands of Sewell's Point, the area that had been infilled to create the toll road from Boston to Brookline (what later became known as Beacon Street). On the left are the Belvoir apartment building and the Peerless Motor Car Company. On the far right is the Hotel Buckminster. Streetcar 923, in the foreground, heads up Commonwealth Avenue; notice the horse trough on the right in the center of the street.

In this view, looking east from Governor's (now Kenmore) Square c. 1903, Commonwealth Avenue has been extended through what Olmstead referred to as the Back Bay Fens. The area was built up with townhouses, large apartment buildings, and hotels, such as the Hotel Somerset (in the center distance, on the edge of Muddy River). The turreted red-brick townhouse on the left was designed by Walker & Kimball and built in 1895. It is now J.S. Waterman & Sons Funeral Home.

Beacon Street intersects Commonwealth Avenue at Governor's Square. A horse-drawn carriage approaches the intersection *c.* 1903, with the Hotel Belvoir, a residential apartment building, on the left. In the distance are townhouses that were built on Bay State Road *c.* 1900 as an extension of Boston's Back Bay, but in an area now referred to as the Back Bay Fens.

The Jenney gasoline station on Commonwealth Avenue at Kenmore Square was designed by Parsons & Wait as a Dutch-influenced building of waterfaced brick with a clock face in colored tile, flanked by gaily decorated shutters under the frontal gable with a belfry surmounted by a cock weathervane. The station was built in 1924, with the ascendancy of the automobile. The first floor had an office with service rooms for both patrons and employees and a porte cochere extending over the fuel pumps in the foreground.

The Fenway Theatre was on Massachusetts Avenue near Boylston Street and had an impressive classical facade with Corinthian pilasters between two-story arched windows supporting a swagged cornice and a roof balustrade that created an impressive addition to the streetscape. The building was designed by Thomas W. Lamb and was built of dark cream glazed Atlantic terra cotta in 1915. The upper floor was leased to Helene L. Sweeney's School of Dancing. On the left is the State Street Bank & Trust Company. Today, the former Fenway Theatre is the Berklee College of Music.

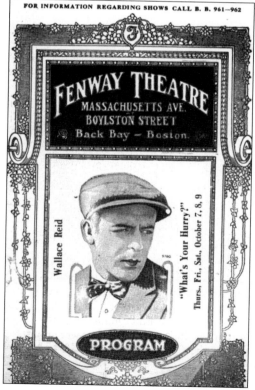

The Fenway Theatre was a leading theater during the age of silent films. Here Wallace Reid is featured as star of *What's Your Hurry?*—part of the October 7, 8, and 9, 1922 program, which started with Lloyd G. del Castillo, organist, leading the overture *Pilgrim's Chorys*, by Wagner. The program also included *Burton Holmes Travel Pictures*, *The Fenway Topical Review*, Geraldine Farrar in *The Woman and the Puppet*, soloist Gerytrude Breene, and the exit march, again by Lloyd G. del Castillo.

Massachusetts Avenue in 1926 had red-brick apartment buildings containing street-level stores that included Charles & David, McMahon & Jacques, Bido's Smoke Shop, Baystate Paint & Hardware. Notice the tower of St. Cecilia's Roman Catholic Church on the upper left.

The new Corinthian-columned portico that was added in 1973 by I.M. Pei Associates to the facade of the First Church of Christ, Scientist adds greatly to the design. With the forecourt cleared of buildings along Massachusetts Avenue, the approach is a splendid vista to the monumental church.

This view of Westland Avenue at Massachusetts Avenue shows Boston's Symphony Hall on the left and the Boston Storage Warehouse on the far right. A streetcar heads south on Massachusetts Avenue as automobiles pull up in front of Symphony Hall on Friday afternoon, one of "the local holy days," when proper Bostonians attend afternoon symphony. Although Symphony Hall is still solidly ensconced on its site, with its ever loyal supporters, the Boston Storage Warehouse was demolished in 1955 and is now the site of Church Park Apartments.

The Boston Storage Warehouse was designed by Chamberlain & Whidden as an early warehouse with small compartments for renters to store possessions on a short- or long-term basis. With its arcaded base that acted as a support for the repetitive bowed arches, it was much more visually interesting than the function for which it was built. On the left, notice the crenelation on the roof and the oriel, both of which connoted security in a castlelike setting for renters' possessions.

In the early 20th century, Hemenway Street was built up with the Conservatory Apartments, which were owned by the New England Conservatory of Music and were for student dormitories. On the left of this view, looking toward Westland Avenue, are the Gardiner, Dana, and Frost Buildings. At the end of the street are the former Trade High School for Girls (left) and the Hemenway Chambers (right).

The Gainsboro Terrace Garden Apartments were a convenient place to live, and the advertisements said that these apartments were adjoining Symphony Hall, the Boston Opera House, the Christian Science Center, and the art museum and that the "rooms are nice and free parking is provided." The red-brick apartments were simple in design and without ornamentation, but the parking lot in the foreground was obviously as much an attraction in 1940 as it is today, considering the space constraints in the Fenway.

Trolley 5121 stops for a truck that has broken down on Ipswich Street near Boylston Street in 1923. The E.A. Patch Company Garage can be seen in the background, with an apartment building on the right. (Courtesy of Frank Cheney.)

Westland Avenue, which runs from Massachusetts Avenue to Hemenway Street, is the entrance to the Fenway. The street was largely built up in the first decade of the 20th century with apartment buildings. In the center can be seen the Johnson Memorial with the Metropolitan District Commission building in the distance.

Trolley 5863 travels along Queensberry Street near Ipswich Street in 1934. Queensbury Street was laid out in 1897 from one end of Audubon Road to the other. Initially, it was envisioned as an area of architect-designed townhouses such as those built on the Fenway, as Robert Treat Paine Jr.'s townhouse, designed by Charles A. Cummings, was built in 1899 at the corner of Queensbury Street and Audubon Road. However, the demographics changed, and after World War I, the area was developed with middle-class apartment buildings. (Courtesy of Frank Cheney.)

Trolley 5891 turns from Massachusetts Avenue onto Boylston Street in 1934. The building on the left, which had a Brigham's ice-cream shop on the first floor, has since been removed due to the extension of the Massachusetts Turnpike. (Courtesy of Frank Cheney.)

The facade of the church facing Massachusetts Avenue rises in 1906, with the framing for the dome being lifted into place. The foundation and base of the church was of granite with the use of Bedford limestone in the construction of the exterior walls of the church.

The St. Paul Street facade of the church presents a classically inspired Byzantine aspect to the area. The expansion of the church also led to increased outreach in the community with the establishment of Christian Science Reading Rooms "for spiritual discovery and exploration" and the *Christian Science Sentinel, Radio Edition* on WXKS AM 1430 and WPBX/PAX TV Channel 68.

An estimated 30,000 members of the Christian Science church streamed into the Mother Church on Dedication Sunday, June 10, 1906, with five identical services held throughout the morning and a noon service especially for children. The difference between the old church, on the right, and the classical extravaganza could not be more obvious. However, what is surprising is the fact that the former was built in 1894 and the latter in 1906. This juxtaposition illustrates how much the church had grown in just over a decade.

The auditorium of the church has seating for 5,000 members and guests of the Christian Science church. With its seven balconies, the interior was revealed without obstruction and with perfect acoustics so that one heard the speaker at the front platform in the rear of the church. The speaker's platform is of soft, grey-white Bedford stone, and the pews are of San Domingo mahogany, with bronze lighting fixtures along the rear and sides of the auditorium and in the balconies.

The speaker's platform and organ in the First Church of Christ, Science is an impressive display of gilded pipes on the east side of the church. The culmination of the church was what Mary Baker Eddy wished, as it is "a magnificent temple wherein to enter and pray."

The organ was composed of approximately 60 feet of gilded pipes, filling the recesses above the reader's platform at the east end of the church. Specifications for the organ were furnished by Albert F. Conant, then organist of the Mother Church, and by the distinguished Boston organist Benjamin J. Lang. The organ had a pure "diapason quality, both in rich timbre and in brilliant mixtures [and] is outstanding and comparable to the foremost cathedral organs of Europe." There is also a melodious chime of bells that has been rung with great pleasure in the past but is not often heard today.

The First Church of Christ, Scientist is a Byzantine design thought to have been inspired by the Mosque of Ahmed I, in Constantinople. The structure presents an impressive sight as seen from Huntington Avenue, between Falmouth, Norway, and St. Paul Streets. The dome, with its arched openings supporting it, created a visual dominance over the area, as its lofty height is 220 feet. By the late 20th century, the Christian Science Church had become an international organization with 2,500 churches, 10,000 practitioners, and an estimated 300,000 members.

The area in the foreground of this view looking from Huntington Avenue was originally a lush lawn, with pruned trees lining walkways and paths. The publishing house wraps around the original church, on the right, and the Mother Church, in the center. The Pulitzer Prize–winning *Christian Science Monitor* is a daily newspaper that was founded by Mary Baker Eddy in 1908, and it specializes in selected and edited news of a nonsensational nature.

Northeastern University's Cabot Physical Education Center occupies the former Huntington Avenue Grounds, a baseball field that was used by the Boston Pilgrims, the forerunners of the Boston Red Sox, until Fenway Park was built. Huntington Avenue, in the foreground, has the Green Line trolley that extends to Brookline, and most of the area has been built up by Northeastern University.

Huntington Avenue was a place where important institutions located to in the early 20th century. On the left is the New England Conservatory of Music, and on the right is the headquarters of the YMCA of Boston.

The New England Conservatory of Music was founded in 1867 in Boston's South End and was "the best equipped school of its kind in America." The impressive school, which also includes Jordan Hall, on Huntington Avenue, was designed by Wheelwright & Haven and has long been considered "one of the greatest institutions of its kind in the country." The entrance hall of the conservatory had the statue of Beethoven, sculpted by Crawford, that was given in trust to the Handel and Haydn Society by Charles C. Perkins. The statue originally stood in the Boston Music Hall on Hamilton Place in downtown Boston.

George W. Chadwick was the director of the New England Conservatory of Music when it moved from Boston's South End to the Fenway. Chadwick was a composer and orchestral conductor of international reputation, and it was due largely to his influence that the school had an average attendance of 3,000 students annually at the turn of the century.

The Leland Powers School of the Spoken Word was founded in 1904; the school was designed by M. Allen Jackson and built in 1914 at the corner of The Fenway and Tetlow Street. Designed in the Colonial style, the red-brick and limestone school had schoolrooms, a reception hall, and a little theater with a seating capacity of 350. The aim of the school was to "train young men and women in all branches of the speech arts, and to fit them both for public platform work and to take charge of Departments of Public Speaking in schools, colleges and universities."

Leland T. Powers (1857–1944) was the founder of the Leland Powers School of the Spoken Word. A graduate of Phillips Academy and the Boston University School of Oratory, Powers became a professional public reader and teacher of the speech arts, or elocution. He was a successful teacher, and his work was "definite, concentrated, practical and personal. The processes of instruction are revelatory and self-discovering, rather than arbitrary and academic, and the work is vocational as well as cultural."

Simmons College was built on the Fenway, next to Isabella Stewart Gardner's impressive home, Fenway Court. Founded in 1899, Simmons College provided instruction for women in such "branches of art, science, and industry" as "best calculated to enable its pupils to acquire an independent livelihood." The school, designed by Peabody & Stearns and built in 1901–1904, was named for John Simmons (1796–1870), a wealthy Boston merchant whose ready-made clothing business was located in the Simmons Block on Water Street in Boston's financial district. After Simmons died in 1870, the bequest was prudently invested until the school was opened in 1899.

The lounge at Simmons College, seen c. 1940, was an inviting place with comfortable sofas and chairs arranged around a large fireplace.

The buildings of the Harvard Medical School were designed by Shepley, Rutan & Coolidge to face onto a large grass forecourt off Longwood Avenue. The buildings were built by Norcross Brothers Company Builders of Dorset, Vermont Plateau white marble from the quarries of Norcross-West Marble Company. The school was to relocate to a vast tract of land in the Longwood section, between Longwood Avenue and Francis Street. Through the generosity of J.P. Morgan and John D. Rockefeller, the five buildings of the Harvard Medical School were devoted to administration, anatomy, histology, bacteriology, and pathology.

The Harvard Medical School, designed by the noted architectural firm of Shepley, Rutan & Coolidge, is considered the center of what was often referred to as the "White City" of buildings constructed of marble. Here, the symmetrically classical building is flanked by side wings and is set back from the street with a large forecourt.

The rear of the Harvard Medical School, located at 25 Shattuck Street, has an impressive facade of Ionic columns supporting a stepped parapet with classical urns.

The garden of the Teachers College of the City of Boston (later known as the Boston State College) can be seen in the foreground with a small glass greenhouse for winter-growing plants. The area of Boston's Fenway also attracted other schools, hospitals, and colleges, such as the Angell Memorial Hospital, the Harvard Medical School, the Children's Hospital, Boston Lying-In Hospital, the Massachusetts College of Pharmacy, and the Latin schools.

Members of the Wentworth Institute baseball team pose in front of the side entrance to the school in 1928. Founded in 1904 as a day and evening school for the study of vocational training and mechanical arts, the school was named for benefactor Arioch Wentworth (1813–1903), a wealthy Boston merchant who funded the school in his will. The school began building its campus in 1913 at the corner of Ruggles Street and Huntington Avenue, opposite the Boston Museum of Fine Arts and opened in 1914 to furnish education in the mechanical arts.

Students at Wentworth learned every aspect of building and the mechanical arts associated with it. Here, in a photograph from 1928, students erect a wood frame to a building they are constructing on the school grounds. These courses in stonework, brick masonry, wood framing, and others prepared the students for their future jobs.

The Mechanic Arts High School of Boston was designed by Edmund March Wheelwright, then city architect of Boston, and built in 1905 on the edge of the railroad yards in Boston's Back Bay. The school, which offered design, mechanical drawing, and drafting to male high school students, was a major feeder to the Massachusetts Institute of Technology, which moved from Boston's Back Bay to Cambridge in 1911. Wheelwright had published *School Architecture* in 1901, which became a treatise for future school architectural design.

The Mechanic Arts High School was impressive in its Romanesque arches that created interest along the four sides of the school, which was punctuated by the tall observatory. The school later moved to Roxbury, where it became known as the Boston Technical High School, an exam school on a par with the Latin schools that offered a concentration on math, science, and drafting. Today, the school is known as the John D. O'Bryant School.

The Boys Latin School (now known as Boston Latin School), designed by the architectural firms of Peabody & Stearns, Maginnis, Walsh & Sullivan and Coolidge & Carlson, was built on Avenue Louis Pasteur in Boston's Fenway. Seen here in an architectural rendering, it had a central building with a cupola flanked by symmetrical buildings. Boston Latin School is a six-year college preparatory school providing a rigorous academic program in the classical tradition. The institution provides the groundwork for full participation in our economy and society. Since its beginning in 1635, school has continued to provide significant opportunities for students to appreciate the importance of education.

The Boston Normal and Girls Latin School, built in 1906–1907, was located at Palace Road, Tetlow Street, and Huntington Avenue. The Girls Latin School eventually relocated to the former Dorchester High School in Dorchester's Codman Square. Today, it is known as Boston Latin Academy and is in the former Roxbury Memorial High School, at the corner of Warren Street and Townsend Avenue in Roxbury.

The Winsor School was designed by noted architect R. Clipston Sturgis (1860–1951) and built in 1909–1910 on Pilgrim Road. The school was founded in 1886 by Mrs. Francis Brooks as a private preparatory school for girls and was taken over a year later by Mary Pickard Winsor, for whom the school was named. An attractive Modern Gothic–style brick school with a belfry and a Doric-columned facade portico, it sits well on its siting adjacent to the Riverway.

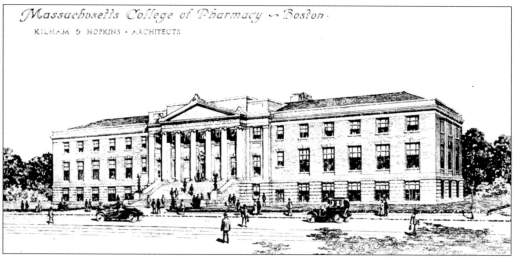

The Massachusetts College of Pharmacy was designed by the noted architectural firm of Kilham & Hopkins and built at 179 Longwood Avenue. Founded in 1823, the college is the second-oldest school of pharmacy in the country but, as is said by the college, is "second to none." The Massachusetts College of Pharmacy and Health Sciences "strives to be a nationally and internationally recognized leader in the education of health professionals." Today, degrees are offered in pharmacy, physician assistance, and nursing.

Eight

MEDICAL

In the late 19th century, Boston led the nation in medical research, and the large number of hospitals established for various specialties was quite impressive. The establishment in 1811 of the Massachusetts General Hospital and the McLean Asylum led the way for new hospitals in the city, among them the Boston City Hospital (1849), the Massachusetts Homoeopathic Hospital (1855), the Carney Hospital (1865), the New England Hospital for Women and Children (1863), the Free Hospital for Women (1875), the Children's Hospital (1869), the Massachusetts Charitable Eye and Ear Infirmary (1824), and numerous smaller hospitals, infirmaries, and medical societies that offered medical assistance to those in need.

However, as Boston grew both in demographics and topography, so too did the need for a wider spectrum of specialty hospitals. The open lands of Boston's Fenway offered not only buildable lots but the promise of future expansion options for hospitals that decided to move to the area. Among these institutions were the Children's Hospital, the Forsyth Dental Infirmary, the Infants' Hospital of the Harvard Medical School, Beth Israel Hospital, and the famous Angell Memorial Hospital, where the beloved pets of Bostonians received their medical attention. Interestingly, the Boston Medical Library moved to the Fenway at the turn of the century. Kept in an impressive headquarters designed by Shaw & Hunnewell were the medical books, journals, and periodicals that could be used by physicians in a central location.

The Boston Medical Library moved from lower Boylston Street to the Fenway at the turn of the century. Founded in 1875 as the Boston Medical Library Association, it had a vast collection of medical reference books both purchased and donated by members for use by local physicians, which proved "of enormous convenience to the medical profession, since information sources are now concentrated in one place." Originally located on Hamilton Place, the library later moved to Boylston Place before the new headquarters, which was designed by the Boston architectural firm of Shaw & Hunnewell and built by McNeil Brothers, was erected in 1890–1891. Today, this is the Boston Conservatory.

Holmes Hall was named for Dr. Oliver Wendell Holmes (1809–1894), the first president of the Boston Medical Library, whose term was from 1875 to 1888. On the left is the portrait of Dr. D. Humphreys Storer, by Frederick Vinton, with framed medals on either side. A bust of Dr. Holmes, sculpted by R.E. Brooks, and his portrait were also located in this room but cannot be seen in the photograph.

The Boston Medical Library was located on the Fenway, near Boylston Street. Known since 1904 as the Warren B. Potter Memorial in recognition of a generous bequest of Sarah E. Potter, widow of Dr. Warren B. Potter, the library was surrounded by equally impressive buildings. On the left is the Fenmore, at the corner of Boylston Street and Charlesgate East. The Massachusetts Historical Society is to the left of the library, and the townhouse of Robert Swain Peabody (1845–1917) is on the right.

John Ware Hall, named for Dr. John Ware, was where the large meetings of the society and the Suffolk District Society were held. The hall was paneled in quarter-sawn oak with ceiling beams overhead. Above the speaker's desk hangs the monumental painting *First Operation under Ether*, by Robert C. Hinckley. The operation took place in 1846 at the Massachusetts General Hospital, and the painting depicts Dr. John Collins Warren operating with the use of ether, which was invented by Dr. Morton. A bust of Dr. Ware by Bela Pratt can be seen on the right, and his portrait is that seen between the two doors.

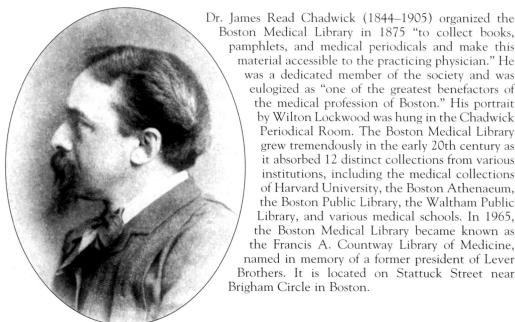

Dr. James Read Chadwick (1844–1905) organized the Boston Medical Library in 1875 "to collect books, pamphlets, and medical periodicals and make this material accessible to the practicing physician." He was a dedicated member of the society and was eulogized as "one of the greatest benefactors of the medical profession of Boston." His portrait by Wilton Lockwood was hung in the Chadwick Periodical Room. The Boston Medical Library grew tremendously in the early 20th century as it absorbed 12 distinct collections from various institutions, including the medical collections of Harvard University, the Boston Athenaeum, the Boston Public Library, the Waltham Public Library, and various medical schools. In 1965, the Boston Medical Library became known as the Francis A. Countway Library of Medicine, named in memory of a former president of Lever Brothers. It is located on Stattuck Street near Brigham Circle in Boston.

The Fifield Room was given to the Boston Medical Library through the generosity of Emily Porter Fifield and her daughter Mary Fifield King in memory of Dr. William Cranch Bond Fifield, a beloved physician who lived in Dorchester. On the left and right walls is a collection of photographs of members of the Dorchester Medical Club, and on the right of the doorway is a portrait of Dr. Cotton Tufts (1736–1815), painted by Benjamin Greenleaf. Dr. Tufts was a physician in Weymouth and was an ancestor of Dr. Fifield.

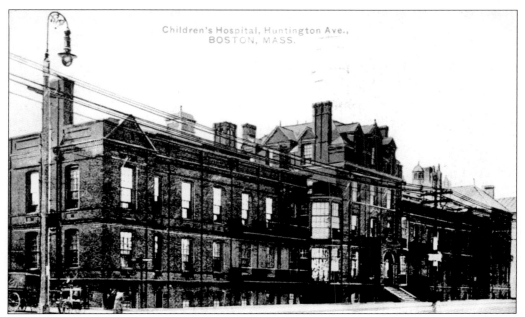

The Children's Hospital was a red-brick and brownstone hospital built between 1881 and 1882 on Huntington Avenue. Founded in 1869, it had originally provided medical attention to children in converted buildings on Washington Street in Boston's South End. In 1914, the hospital moved from this building to Longwood Avenue, and this impressive building was demolished three years later.

The Children's Hospital moved to the corner of Longwood Avenue and Vila Street in Boston's Fenway in 1914. The hospital was designed by Shepley, Rutan & Coolidge with a temple-fronted building with a center dome. Today, the Children's Hospital has been rated first in child care annually since 1980 and offers some of the best pediatric care in the world.

The classic exterior of the Forsyth Dental Infirmary can be seen through the lush greenery of the Fens. In the foreground, a part of Olmstead's Emerald Necklace acts as a natural softening to the classical lines of the building, which was built in memory of James Bennett Forsyth (1850–1909) and George Henry Forsyth (1854–1906), co-owners with their brothers John Hamilton and Thomas A. Forsyth, of the Boston Belting Company. James and George Forsyth bequeathed a $2 million endowment for a dental infirmary for children with additional funds for the erection and equipping of a building that stands as a noble monument to their generosity.

The Dental Hygienists' Clinic at the Forsyth Dental Infirmary had a class for hygienists for children who do not require the attention of dentists; the School for Dental Hygiene was opened in 1916. The infirmary continues to offer dental care to children whose parents are often unable to meet the expense of dental care. The institution sought to make people aware of the essential relationship between dental hygiene and the general health of the person. "All children of Greater Boston, either poor or moderately circumstanced, are eligible to free treatments here by a corps of trained dentists, sixty-four working at a time at as many chairs, while there is room for a second row of forty-four chairs to meet growing demands.".

The Forsyth Dental Infirmary for Children was designed by architect Edward T.P. Graham and is located at 140 The Fenway. Through the generosity of the Forsyth Brothers of Roxbury, "the teeth of all those children whose parents earn only a certain limited sum a week, will be cared for in a wonderfully equipped infirmary." It was said that in 1911, the Boston Board of Health found that out of 180,781 Boston schoolchildren, 51,340 had defective teeth, while nearly as many more suffered from related troubles. "Good teeth mean good health, hence the influence of this institution upon future generations. . . . Its founders have the city's unalloyed gratitude." The clinic was in full operation by January 1915, and shortly thereafter, a school of orthodontia was established.

A dental hygienist leads the "toothbrush drill" for children to become familiar the custom of daily oral hygiene. The Oral Hygiene Department offered direction to children for daily brushing and flossing and care of teeth that precluded loss by indifference. Traveling dental clinics often went to schools and settlement houses to expound about the care of teeth by children. The infirmary was hygienic throughout, with walls and ceilings covered in glazed tiles produced by the Grueby and Paul Revere Potteries. A children's waiting room was decorated with a mural of colored tiles representing legends and fairy tales. The bronze doors at the entrance to the infirmary were sculpted by Roger N. Burham.

The Beth Israel Hospital was founded in 1917 to serve the needs of primarily Jewish patients in Boston's Roxbury neighborhood. Today, a century after its founding, the hospital is located in the Fenway and is known as the Beth Israel Deaconess Medical Center, which offers patient care and training for Harvard Medical School students—a fact that confirms the hospital's commitment to the "health and well-being of people in our region."

The Infants' Hospital of the Harvard Medical School is a place where "cases of Infantile Paralysis and other infantile diseases" are brought. Operated by Harvard University, care is offered to children with the parents paying for treatments received. If one could not afford the medical services offered, there was the Boston City Hospital and the Floating Hospital for Children, both of which offered low cost, or in some cases free medical care for children.

The headquarters of the Massachusetts Society for the Prevention of Cruelty to Animals (MSPCA) was located on Longwood Avenue in an impressive classical red-brick and limestone building (designed by Putnam and Cox), where medical attention is offered for the animals of Boston. Here, in the Angell Memorial Hospital, the care "for animals, large and small, pets and strays" is offered in clean stalls and white cages. Angell's philosophy was "Be Kind to Animals," which extended from workhorses and strays to beloved family pets. The phrase was also written into the pavement leading into the courtyard so all could ponder his benevolent words as they passed.

George Thorndike Angell (1823–1909) devoted much of his life to humane work of all kinds, but his primary focus was for the welfare of animals. He founded the MSPCA and the American Humane Education Society and, in 1868, began the publication of *Our Dumb Animals,* a widely read newspaper and the first of its kind in the world. A graduate of Brown and Dartmouth as well as a successful attorney in Boston, Angell devoted more than four decades of his life to bettering the life of animals. The city of Boston erected a monument to his dedication to the plight of animals in Post Office Square; this monument was designed by Peabody & Stearns and is in Angell Memorial Park in Post Office Square, which was designed by Earl Flansburgh and Associates.

Baseball fans line up outside Fenway Park before a game in the 1920s, with mounted Boston police officers overseeing the crowds. After it was built in 1912, Fenway Park attracted a larger attendance than that of the old Huntington Avenue Grounds, which had few amenities. Fenway Park was built on 365,308 square feet of land with stadium seating and fairly comfortable amenities. Built of red brick and patterned after Shibe Park in Philadelphia, Fenway Park was designed by architect James E. McLaughlin as a building of tapestry brick in a modified Colonial style. It incorporates such details as diamond patterns in brick and decorative mosaics.

Carl Yastrezemski poses at Fenway Park before a game, holding a "Genuine Carl Yastrezemski Louisville Slugger." Born in New York in 1939, "Yaz" was to succeed Ted Williams in the left field at Fenway Park in 1961. A plaque erected in his honor at Fenway Park reads, "[He] played with graceful intensity in record 3,308 American League games. Only American League player with 3,000 hits and 400 homers, 3-time batting champion. Won MVP and Triple Crown in 1967 as he led Red Sox to 'Impossible Dream' Pennant." Yastrezemski was inducted into the National Baseball Hall of Fame in Cooperstown, New York, on July 23, 1989, and his Red Sox baseball uniform (No. 8) was retired that same year.

Nine

FENWAY PARK
AND THE RED SOX

Baseball began in 1839 in Cooperstown, New York, when a group of students from the Otsego Academy played a game of town ball against students from Green's Select School. The rules of town ball were so ambiguous that almost every hit was considered fair, with the players often making up the rules as they went along. However, it was Abner Doubleday, a member of the Otsego Academy team, who drew up a list of rules pertaining to the game and christened it "baseball," thereby creating a new American pastime that is enjoyed by some and fanatically followed by others to this day.

In 1901, the Boston Pilgrims became a charter member of the American League and played ball at the Huntington Avenue Grounds, now a part of Northeastern University. The team was bought in 1904 by Gen. Charles H. Taylor, publisher of the *Boston Globe,* and was given as a gift to his son John I. Taylor, who in 1907 renamed his club the Boston Red Sox. John I. Taylor decided that he would build a stadium for his team, and he named it Fenway Park because of its location in the Back Bay Fens. The Taylor family owned extensive tracts of land in the former wetlands of the Back Bay Fens under the Fenway Realty Company. The opening game in the new park, which was the third largest in the country, was on April 20, 1912, when the Red Sox defeated the New York Highlanders (later known as the Yankees) in front of 27,000 fans.

Although Fenway Park has been synonymous with the Boston Red Sox since it was built, it has also hosted such non-baseball events as the final campaign speech of Franklin Delano Roosevelt in 1944, the College Baseball Beanpot, fundraisers for the Jimmy Fund, the Adopt a Kid program for the Massachusetts Department of Social Services, and other fundraisers for charities. Novelist John Updike once wrote that Fenway Park represents "a compromise between Man's Euclidean determinations and Nature's beguiling irregularities." However the park is perceived, one thing is certain—it is Boston's playland.

Members of the Boston Red Sox pose in front of the bleachers at Fenway Park on August 19,

The Boston Red Sox participate in a game of the 1903 World Series at the old Huntington Avenue Grounds. Notice the packed bleachers in the distance, but with hundreds of sports afficionados lining the outer edge of the baseball field in the foreground as well as sitting on top of the fence to see the game better. The high wood-planked perimeter wall was lined, both inside and out, with advertisements—a practice that continues today. The site of the old baseball field is now Northeastern University's Cabot Physical Education Center.

1914. The umpire in the middle holds the team's mascot, appropriately a Boston terrier.

Gen. Charles Henry Taylor (1846–1921) was editor in chief, general manager, and (later) publisher of the *Boston Globe*. He bought the Boston Red Sox franchise at a price "close to $150,000" and presented the team as a gift to his son, John Irving Taylor (1875–1938). John I. Taylor (seen here) owned the Red Sox from 1904 to 1912, but the team was managed by Jimmy Collins, who was often at odds with Taylor. In 1907, Taylor appointed former center fielder Chick Stahl as manager, but Stahl's subsequent suicide produced problems, and Taylor sold the team in 1912 to James McAleer. (Private collection.)

119

Members of the Boston Red Sox pose for a victory photograph at Fenway Park after having become the world champions in 1912. During the 1911–1912 season, the Red Sox won 105 games and were victorious over the New York Giants in the World Series. Among the baseball players were Wagner, Henricksen, Hooper, Lewis, Ball, Collins, Janvrin, Speaker, Nuntismaker, Engle, Foster, Cady, O'Brien, Thomas, Gardner, Yerkes, Hall, Bedient, Wood, Carrigan, and Leonard.

The great Babe Ruth signs autographs for fans at Fenway Park. A member of the Boston Red Sox from 1914 to 1919, the Babe (George Herman Ruth) was traded to the New York Giants. He was known for his legendary swing and has often been called the best baseball player of all time and one with the most recognizable of names.

Members of the world champion Boston Red Sox pose at Fenway Park on September 15, 1915. From left to right are "Sad Sam" Jones, Carl Mays, Babe Ruth, and Les Nunsmaker at the opening game of the 1915 World Series.

In this October 14, 1915 photograph, a beaming William Carrigan, Boston Red Sox manager, holds a check in the amount of $86,939.73, payable from the Federal Trust Company for the team's share of the 1915 World Series. Each member of the Boston Red Sox was to receive $3,951.80 for his efforts.

Manager Edward Barrows (left) and pitcher Sad Sam Jones of the Boston Red Sox enjoy a lighthearted exchange in the bullpen just prior to the fourth game of the 1918 World Series. The game, which pitted the Boston Red Sox against the Chicago Cubs, was held on September 9, 1918, at Fenway Park.

Fenway Park, seen here in 1914, was designed by James E. McLaughlin and was built in 1912 on marshland called the Back Bay Fens, which eventually translated into the Fenway. The Osborn Engineering Company provided civil engineering services, and the stadium was built by the Charles Logue Building Company. Fenway Park was opened on April 20, 1912, and the team abandoned the old Huntington Avenue Grounds, which had been leased. In 1937, park renovations included the replacement of the wooden wall with a 37-foot wall made of 2-inch steel. Fenway Park was once described by poet David Hall as being "like a huge pinball machine designed by a mad sculptor."

These boys, some with their lunch and roasted peanuts in brown paper bags, await the call for bleacher seats on opening day in 1956. Former Speaker of the House of Representatives Edward "Tip" O'Neill once commented on the sincere "chumminess of the ballpark. It's like being in an English theatre. You're right on top of the stage." One hopes that these young baseball fans had not played hooky to attend this game at Fenway Park.

Baseball fans line up along Brookline Avenue and Jersey Street (now renamed Yawkey Way) in 1948 to purchase tickets at the advance sales office at Fenway Park. What is interesting is that the baseball fans are from all aspects of society—different sexes, ages, and races—but all are in hopes of tickets to an enjoyable baseball game. Once described as the collective place "where memories are stored," Fenway Park represents a time capsule, not just in architecture and design of the early 20th century but also as the one place that remains virtually unchanged in the city.

Joe DiMaggio is seen hitting a pitch at a game at Fenway Park in 1937. An all-time great baseball player, DiMaggio was a member of the New York Yankees, but his brother Dom DiMaggio was a member of the Boston Red Sox.

The Boston Red Sox were the 1946 American League champions, and they pose for a group photograph in Fenway Park. Among the players are Rudy York, Bobby Doerr, Johnny Pesky, R. Russell, C. Metkovich, Dom DiMaggio, Ted Williams, Charlie Wagner, P. Higgins, L. Culberson, W. Moses, Tex Hughson, B. Ferriss, Bucky Harris, J. Dobson, Jim Bagby, E. Johnson, and B. Klinger. Manager Joe Cronin is in the back row on the far right.

John Fitzgerald Kennedy (1919–1963), third from the left, admires Hank Greenberg's bat at a ballgame between the Boston Red Sox and the Detroit Tigers at Fenway Park in 1946. Looking on are Ted Williams and Eddie Pellagrini of the Boston Red Sox. Kennedy was campaigning for a seat in the Massachusetts House of Representatives. His victory in that race led to his election to the Senate and, eventually, to the presidency.

The August 20, 1934 ball game at Fenway Park was packed with fans. In this view from the rear of the grandstands, the excitement of the day is obvious, with everyone awaiting the next pitch. In 1936, to protect the windows of buildings adjoining Fenway Park, a tall sheet-metal screen replaced an earlier wood wall in left field. When renovations were undertaken in 1947, including the addition of park lights, the wall's advertisements were painted over in green paint, and the "Green Monster" was christened.

Members of the All-Star teams, the American League, and the National League line up along the baselines at Fenway Park before the Midsummer Classic of 1961. The band plays "The Star-Spangled Banner" as the baseball players and audience stand at attention. Note the clock surmounting the billboard. The advertisement below it reads, "Remember the Jimmy Fund." The game, ending a 1-1 tie, was called after nine innings on account of rain.

Don Mattingly (left) of the New York Mets and Wade Boggs of the Boston Red Sox compare whose bat has seen more action in a game at Fenway Park in 1983. During his 11 years with the Red Sox (1974–1985), Boggs averaged .338, getting more than 200 hits in seven straight seasons. Boggs left the Red Sox for the Yankees.

126

In the 1980s, Fenway Park was considered not just a historic baseball park but a part of American culture. Although some parts of the park have been modernized since it was built in 1912, it today remains as an aging structure that has major limitations when compared to more modern parks. However, the Green Monster is paramount in the preservation plans, which ensure that Fenway Park remains as a time capsule. In the distance, between flanking floodlights, is the Citgo gas sign, a neon advertising board that was saved in 1983 by a determined group of preservationists. Hopefully, other preservationists will ensure that Fenway Park is here for our descendants to enjoy, just like our grandparents did in the early 20th century.

One of the biggest fans of the Boston Red Sox was Dick Casey (1894–1981) of Dorchester. In this photograph, he throws out the first ball at the opening game at Fenway Park on August 10, 1981. Casey was a baseball player himself and was once a member of the Catholic League, the Boston Braves, the Twin State League, and the Boston Twilight League. In 1925, he was elected to the House of Representatives, serving from the Neponset section of Dorchester. His mentoring included the All-Star Baseball League, which preceded the Dick Casey Club, a part of the Boston Park League, which was to win 11 championships in 17 years. The BoSox Club, of which he served as president, honored him in 1969 with the "Mr. Sandlot Baseball Since 1912" award. In 1971, he was given Ambassador of Baseball honors by the city of Boston. He was also awarded the Fanny Award by Sport Huddle (1974) and the Brad Jernegan Award by the BoSox Club (1976). In 1982, he was elected to the Boston Park League Hall of Fame.

The Boston Pilgrims (soon to be rechristened the Boston Red Sox, whose red socks became their trademark) won the first World Series (1903). The Boston Pilgrims met the Pittsburgh Pirates at the Huntington Avenue Grounds in the Fenway of Boston, where they achieved victory. Here, in an assortment of uniforms but with each player sporting red socks, they pose for a celebratory photograph.

Acknowledgments

Thanks go to those who contributed either directly or indirectly in the research, writing, and editing of this photographic history: Jill Anderson, editor at Arcadia Publishing; the Bernard Casey family; Elise Ciregna and Stephen Lo Piccolo; Rupert A.M. Davis; Dexter; Edward W. Gordon; Jack Grinold; James Z. Kyprianos; Susan Wood Paine, president of the Museum of Fine Arts; Rev. Michael J. Parise; J.B. Price; Anthony and Mary Mitchell Sammarco; Robert G. Stone, who introduced the author to the Fenway over two decades ago; Anne and George Thompson; the Urban College of Boston; William Varrell; and Virginia M. White. Unless otherwise noted, photographs are from the author's collection.